Bible Stories
for Grown-Ups:
Leader Guide

Bible Stories for Grown-Ups
Reading Scripture with New Eyes

Bible Stories for Grown-Ups
978-1-7910-2662-2
978-1-7910-2663-9 *eBook*

Bible Stories for Grown-Ups: DVD
978-1-7910-2666-0

Bible Stories for Grown-Ups: Leader Guide
978-1-7910-2664-6
978-1-7910-2665-3 *eBook*

Josh Scott

Bible Stories for Grown-Ups

READING SCRIPTURE WITH NEW EYES

─── **LEADER GUIDE** ───
by Mike Poteet

Abingdon Press | Nashville

Bible Stories for Grown-Ups:
Reading Scripture with New Eyes
Leader Guide

MANUFACTURED IN THE UNITED STATES OF AMERICA

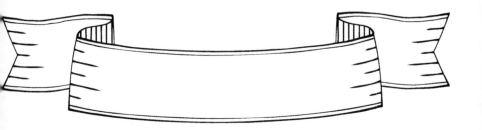

Contents

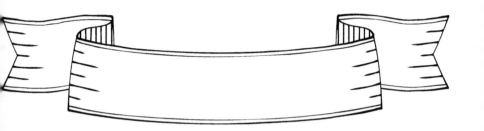

Introduction

In *Bible Stories for Grown-Ups*, Josh Scott, Lead Pastor of GracePointe Church in Nashville, Tennessee, invites and challenges readers to revisit Bible stories familiar to many Christians, reading them through unfamiliar—and perhaps sometimes uncomfortable—"lenses."

Josh explains that everyone reads Scripture through multiple sets of interpretive "lenses," some of which were appropriate when we were children and may still be appropriate for children today, but which can keep grown-ups from appreciating, understanding, and applying biblical truths in all their complexity and richness.

Despite claims to the contrary, no one "just reads" the Bible, as Josh argues. Instead, we can all name the lenses through which we read Scripture and, as necessary, try to refine or replace those lenses "as we learn and grow."

This Leader's Guide is designed to help adult study and discuss *Bible Stories for Grown-Ups* in group Christian education settings. A group leader will want to read Josh's book to lead this study most effectively and should encourage participants to read it, as well. However, recognizing the fact that not all participants may have access to the book or the time to read it, this Leader's Guide carefully follows the content of Josh's book and includes several quotations from it, allowing all participants to find value in the study on their own.

Each session in this Leader Guide covers one chapter from Josh's book, and includes these sections:

- **Session Objectives** state the desired goals of each session and can guide leaders as they choose study questions and activities from the lesson plan, or design their own.
- **Biblical Foundations** present key Scriptures for each chapter in the New Revised Standard Version, Updated Edition.
- **Before Your Session:** This section presents things leaders will want to do before each session to facilitate a smooth and productive experience for the group.
- **Starting Your Session:** This section presents "icebreakers," discussion starters, or other approaches to the session topic and initial conversation.
- **Engaging the Story:** This section can guide your group's initial hearing of and responses to each session's Bible story or stories. The questions encourage participants to encounter the Bible stories as stories, before bringing other concerns and commitments to the discussion.
- **Watch the Video:** Your group may choose to inform and enhance its discussion with the video segments accompanying Bible Stories for Grown-Ups, available on DVD or through Amplify Media.
- **Exploring the Story:** This section encourages deeper engagement with the biblical story, drawing heavily from material Josh presents in his book.
- **Closing Your Session:** This section encourages participants to apply questions and issues Josh raises in each chapter of Bible Stories for Grown-Ups to not only their own experience but also their congregation's life together.
- **Opening Prayers and Closing Prayers** are provided for leaders who wish to use prepared prayers in their sessions, although leaders may also choose to pray extemporaneously and in their own words.

You will likely not be able to use all the questions provided in the lesson plans. Use your knowledge of your group to help you choose and use the ones you think will benefit them most. Leaders should always be ready to model willing and honest discussion by answering first any questions they pose to the group. The sessions are not written for participants who are unwilling to talk!

What stories will groups read in new ways in this study?

- **Session 1** covers the Flood narratives in Genesis. Are they simply cute tales of a floating zoo and a rainbow? What do they tell us about human violence, as well as human responsibility for shaping and reshaping God's creation?
- **Session 2** shines a light on one of the Bible's most disturbing stories, Abraham's near-sacrifice of his son, Isaac. How does this traumatic tale challenge our ideas not only about obedience to God but also the very nature of God?
- **Session 3** recounts the story of Jonah. The "big fish" that swallowed him gets a lot of press, but what does Scripture's most reluctant and stubborn prophet show us about God's will for responding to our enemies?
- **Session 4** reintroduces us to parables—the brief, fictional stories Jesus told to illuminate the kingdom of heaven— and explores in detail the parable of the talents. Is this story a picture of what God is like—or a summons to resist what our society is like?
- **Session 5** considers the story of Jesus's encounter with the tax collector Zacchaeus. We usually remember him as a "wee little man," but the great big change his meeting with Jesus prompted is where the tale's true significance is found.
- **Session 6** examines two miracles attributed to Jesus in Mark 8–9: the healing of a man who was blind, and the exorcism of an unclean spirit. Why did Jesus perform

miracles? Why did he, according to Mark, try to keep his identity as Messiah a secret? And how do these ancient stories inform our attitudes toward being Jesus's disciples today?

Thank you for leading your group in this study of *Bible Stories for Grown-Ups*. May God bless your preparation and your leading as you give this gift of time and energy to help build up the body of Christ, "until all of us come to the unity of the faith and of the knowledge of the Son of God, to maturity, to the measure of the full stature of Christ" (Ephesians 4:13)—in other words, until we are completely "grown up" in God's sight!

SESSION 1

Preventing the Flood: The Story of Noah

SESSION OBJECTIVES

This session's readings and discussions will help participants:

- Remember and reflect on their childhood engagement with Bible stories.
- Begin identifying "lenses" through which they read and interpret Scripture and name elements of a "grown-up lens" for reading the Bible.
- Hear, read, and respond to the Flood story in Genesis 6–9 in new ways, paying special attention to human and divine responsibility in the story.
- Name possible "arks" that could provide us and the world safe passage to a better future today.

BIBLICAL FOUNDATIONS

The LORD saw that the wickedness of humans was great in the earth and that every inclination of the thoughts of their hearts was only evil continually. And the LORD was sorry that he had made humans on the earth, and it grieved him to his heart. So the L*ORD* said, "I will blot out from the earth the humans I have created—people together with animals and creeping things and birds of the air—for I am sorry that I have made them." But Noah found favor in the sight of the L*ORD*.

Genesis 6:5-8

The flood continued forty days on the earth, and the waters increased and bore up the ark, and it rose high above the earth. The waters swelled and increased greatly on the earth, and the ark floated on the face of the waters. The waters swelled so mightily on the earth that all the high mountains under the whole heaven were covered; the waters swelled above the mountains, covering them fifteen cubits deep. And all flesh died that moved on the earth, birds, domestic animals, wild animals, all swarming creatures that swarm on the earth, and all human beings; everything on dry land in whose nostrils was the breath of life died. He blotted out every living thing that was on the face of the ground, human beings and animals and creeping things and birds of the air; they were blotted out from the earth. Only Noah was left and those with him in the ark. And the waters swelled on the earth for one hundred fifty days.

Genesis 7:17-24

Then God said to Noah, "Go out of the ark, you and your wife and your sons and your sons' wives with you. Bring out with you every living thing that is with you of all flesh—birds and animals and every creeping thing that creeps on the earth—so that they may abound on the earth and be fruitful and multiply on the earth." So Noah went out with his sons and his wife and his sons' wives. And every animal, every creeping thing, and every bird, everything that moves on the earth, went out of the ark by families.

Then Noah built an altar to the L*ORD* and took of every clean animal and of every clean bird and offered burnt offerings on the altar. And when the L*ORD* smelled the pleasing odor, the L*ORD* said in his heart, "I will never again curse the ground because *of humans, for the inclination of the human heart is evil from youth; nor will I ever again destroy every living creature as I have done."*

Genesis 8:15-21

Then God said to Noah and to his sons with him, "As for me, I am establishing my covenant with you and your descendants after you and with every living creature that is with you, the birds, the domestic animals, and every animal of the earth with you, as many as came out of the ark. I establish my covenant with you, that never again shall all flesh be cut off by the waters of a flood, and never again shall there be a flood to destroy the earth."

God said, "This is the sign of the covenant that I make between me and you and every living creature that is with you, for all future generations: I have set my bow in the clouds, and it shall be a sign of the covenant between me and the earth."

Genesis 9:8-13

BEFORE YOUR SESSION

- Carefully read the Introduction and chapter 1 of *Bible Stories for Grown-Ups*. Note topics about which you have questions or want to do further research.
- Read Genesis 6:5–9:17 several times, as well as background information from a trusted study Bible or commentary.
- Preview the session 1 video segment. Make notes to facilitate your group's discussion of it. Test your audiovisual equipment and/or capabilities for sharing your videoconference screen.
- You will need: Bibles for participants and/or on-screen slides to share, prepared with the biblical text; newsprint or markerboard; markers.
- *Optional*: Acquire or borrow a flannelgraph board and figures to show to your group. Check your own or neighboring churches or online retailers.

STARTING YOUR SESSION

Welcome participants, and thank them for joining you in this study of *Bible Stories for Grown-Ups* by Josh Scott. Tell them why you wanted to lead this study and ask them to talk briefly about what they hope to gain from it.

Summarize Josh's childhood experience of flannelgraphs (see his Introduction). Discuss:

- What are your earliest memories of hearing and telling Bible stories?
- Josh writes the flannelgraph may now seem "a limited and primitive approach to storytelling, but in those childhood days…[using it] brought the stories of the Bible to life in brand-new ways." Which adults, if any, brought Bible stories "to life" for you when you were younger, and how?
- How did or does your childhood engagement with Bible stories influence your attitudes toward the Bible today?
- How does your congregation attempt to bring Bible stories "to life" for young people? How do you evaluate whether it is succeeding?

Optional: If you have a flannelgraph board and figures to show your group, do so.

Tell participants Josh asks readers whether they've heard people say, "I'm just telling you what the Bible says," but that "[i]t just isn't true…[T]he moment we begin talking about what a passage of the Bible means, we are now firmly in the realm of interpretation." Discuss:

- Do you agree with Josh's claim? Why or why not?
- Josh says "we all bring lenses" to reading the Bible— "layers and layers of experiences and classes and sermons that, over time, [serve] to create an interpretation." How do or how might we become aware of "lenses" through which we read the Bible?

- How, if at all, can these factors affect our "lenses" for reading Scripture: Gender? Ethnicity? Family background? Economic situation? Sexual orientation? Political affiliations? Religious tradition?
- What does or could happen if we mistake the "lenses" through which we read the Bible for the Bible itself? What do or can we do to avoid or mitigate that mistake?
- How is reading and interpreting the Bible like and/or unlike reading and interpreting other literature?

Write on markerboard or newsprint (or share a prepared slide listing) the elements of a "grown-up lens" Josh identifies:

1. Curiosity
2. Taking the Bible seriously, not always literally
3. Paying attention to a story's historical and biblical contexts
4. Applying the Bible's meanings to our own contexts

As you list each of these elements, ask participants if they agree it is important for reading the Bible as adults, and why or why not. After listing all four, ask participants to name other qualities, if any, they think belong in a "grown-up lens" for reading Scripture.

OPENING PRAYER

God, we gather to read, discuss, and reflect on ancient stories created by our spiritual ancestors who lived so long ago. These stories are familiar to us, yet we long to hear them in a fresh way that explores and honors the context in which they were created; and yet, we also hope to hear what the challenges they present can say to us in our own time and place. Help us remain open and responsive, we pray. Amen.

ENGAGING THE FLOOD STORY

If time permits, have volunteers read aloud Genesis 6:9–9:17, which contain both Flood narratives in full. If time is limited, recruit volunteers to read aloud this session's Biblical Foundations, one after the other, while everyone else listens. Ask those who aren't reading aloud to keep their Bibles closed for the time being. Alternatively, listen together to a recorded reading of these chapters.

After the reading(s), discuss:

- What are your immediate reactions to and dominant impressions of the Flood story in Genesis?
- What language or images affected you most strongly, and why?
- Identify and briefly describe each major character in this story.
- What moment in this story do you identify as most important? Why?
- If asked to give this story a title, what would you title it?

WATCH THE VIDEO

Watch the session 1 video segment via DVD or Amplify Media. Invite responses and comments.

EXPLORING THE FLOOD STORY

Invite participants to open their Bibles to Genesis 6–9. Discuss:

- Josh states "the idea of catastrophic flooding was a fairly common concern and focus in the ancient world," citing the ancient Gilgamesh epic as one example. How do you account for similarities between the Flood material and other ancient stories?

- Find some examples of the differences (names for God, number of animals, length of the Flood, type of bird Noah sends) that led Bible scholars to conclude the Flood material originally came from different narrative sources. How do you react to this idea? How, if at all, does it affect your understanding of and attitude toward Scripture?

- The Flood story depicts "human beings on the brink of extinction as a direct result of their preoccupation with violence," writes Josh. What do the consequences of violence in this story show us about humanity? How like or unlike humanity before the Flood would you say humanity is today, and why? Do you think "the inclination of the human heart is evil from youth" (8:21)? Why or why not?

- Josh connects the Flood story to the earlier story of Cain and Abel. Read this story in Genesis 4:1-16. Why does this story present sin, as Josh notes, "as something that is singular" rather than plural (verse 7)? How does this concept of sin shape the way we understand the situation in Genesis 6, and God's response to it? To what extent do you relate to this concept of sin, and why?

- "Violence isn't just something that takes place on a macro level," writes Josh, "and it isn't always physical." When and where do you see nonphysical violence on the personal, "micro" level? What do you tend to do about it? How does your faith shape your response to such violence?

- The Flood story is a tale of human violence. To what extent, if any, is it also one of divine violence? The "bow" God sets in the clouds (9:13)—the colorful rainbow on the covers of children's Bibles—is a weapon. On the other hand, as Josh notes, "the cause of the catastrophic collapse of the sky" in this story—the unraveling of God's creation—"was human violence." How much responsibility does God bear for the Flood, and why?

- Josh suggests the Flood story reflects our "spiritual ancestors" struggling to develop ideas about God, humanity, and the world that differed from those held by other ancient cultures. If you had only the Flood story in Genesis, what might you think and believe about God? How do other Scriptures you know confirm and/or challenge the Flood story's presentation of God?

- "Our ancestors learned that God doesn't act out of annoyance," writes Josh. "Perhaps we are learning that God doesn't respond to our human violence with global violence, but with love and compassion." Do you agree? Why or why not?

- The Flood story ends with God making "the Noahic covenant" with Noah and his family—as Josh writes, "a promise from God to all humanity that never again would this kind of deluge happen." How are Genesis 8:20-22 and 9:1-17 similar and different in narrating God's promises to Noah and humanity? What can we infer from these promises about all human beings' relationship to God and to each other?

CLOSING YOUR SESSION

Read aloud from *Bible Stories for Grown-Ups*: "…Noah and his family are provided with an ark to guide them through the Flood and into a new future.…[W]hat might the arks available to us look like?" Discuss:

- What possible "arks" does Josh identify? How, specifically, have you seen each of them carry an individual or a community into a new and better future?

- What other "arks," if any, would you add to Josh's list, and why?

- Josh professes optimism that we can "turn the tide and avoid our own Great Flood." Do you share this optimism? Why or why not?

CLOSING PRAYER

God, may we learn the lessons of the time of Noah. We live in a world awash in violence. We regularly hear reports of people and nations using our technology and creativity to harm one another, instead of healing. Give us the wisdom and courage to seek the Way of Jesus that calls us to lay down our weapons and love our enemies. As we follow the Spirit may we do our part to stem the rising waters that threaten our shared existence and, instead, pursue love, empathy, peace, and justice, we pray. Amen.

SESSION 2

A New Vision of God: The Binding of Isaac

SESSION OBJECTIVES

This session's readings and discussions will help participants:

- Broadly review the story of Abraham, acknowledging his status as a foundational figure in Judaism, Christianity, and Islam.
- Hear, read, and respond to the story of the binding of Isaac (Genesis 22:1-19) in new ways, paying special attention to difficult questions it raises about what constitutes faithful obedience to God.
- Consider how God may be inviting them to change their minds about God, and what practical difference such changes might make for themselves and others.

BIBLICAL FOUNDATION

After these things God tested Abraham. He said to him, "Abraham!" And he said, "Here I am." He said, "Take your son, your only son Isaac, whom you love, and go to the land of Moriah and offer him there as a burnt offering on one of the mountains that I shall show you." So Abraham rose early in the morning, saddled his donkey, and took two of his young men with him and his son Isaac; he cut the wood for the burnt offering and set out and went to the place in the distance that God had shown him. On the third day Abraham looked up and saw the place far away. Then Abraham said to his young men, "Stay here with the donkey; the boy and I will go over there; we will worship, and then we will come back to you." Abraham took the wood of the burnt offering and laid it on his son Isaac, and he himself carried the fire and the knife. And the two of them walked on together. Isaac said to his father Abraham, "Father!" And he said, "Here I am, my son." He said, "The fire and the wood are here, but where is the lamb for a burnt offering?" Abraham said, "God himself will provide the lamb for a burnt offering, my son." And the two of them walked on together.

When they came to the place that God had shown him, Abraham built an altar there and laid the wood in order. He bound his son Isaac and laid him on the altar on top of the wood. Then Abraham reached out his hand and took the knife to kill his son. But the angel of the LORD called to him from heaven and said, "Abraham, Abraham!" And he said, "Here I am." He said, "Do not lay your hand on the boy or do anything to him, for now I know that you fear God, since you have not withheld your son, your only son, from me." And Abraham looked up and saw a ram, caught in a thicket by its horns. Abraham went and took the ram and offered it up as a burnt offering instead of his son. So Abraham called that place "The LORD will provide," as it is said to this day, "On the mount of the LORD it shall be provided."

The angel of the LORD called to Abraham a second time from heaven and said, "By myself I have sworn, says the LORD: Because you have done this, and have not withheld your son, your only son, I will indeed bless you, and I will make your offspring as numerous as the stars of heaven and as the sand that is on the seashore. And your offspring shall possess the gate of their enemies, and by your offspring shall all the nations of the *earth gain blessing for themselves, because you have obeyed my voice." So Abraham returned to his young men, and they arose and went together to Beer-sheba, and Abraham lived at Beer-sheba.*

Genesis 22:1-19

BEFORE YOUR SESSION

- Carefully read chapter 2 of *Bible Stories for Grown-Ups*. Note topics about which you have questions or want to do further research.
- Read Genesis 22:1-19 several times, as well as background information from a trusted study Bible or commentary.
- Preview the session 2 video segment. Make notes to facilitate your group's discussion of it. Test your audiovisual equipment and/or capabilities for sharing your videoconference screen.
- You will need: Bibles for participants and/or on-screen slides to share, prepared with the biblical text; newsprint or markerboard; markers.

STARTING YOUR SESSION

Welcome participants. Recruit a volunteer to read aloud Genesis 12:1-4. Read aloud from *Bible Stories for Grown-Ups*: "That setting out and leaving behind cement Abraham's place as the father of three major world religions [Judaism, Christianity, and Islam] and make him the poster-human for what faith looks like in practice for billions of people."

Lead participants in brainstorming a list of what they know about Abraham. Write responses on markerboard or newsprint.

Tell participants this session explores a story about Abraham that is far less fun than the "Father Abraham" song. It is a story called in Hebrew the Akedah (pronounced "ah-keh-DAH"), or "binding," because in it, Abraham binds his son on an altar and almost kills him. Tell participants this is a "grown-up" story—and in this session, your group will attempt to read and interpret it through a "grown-up" lens.

OPENING PRAYER

God, we acknowledge that so many of us struggle with the story of Abraham's near sacrifice of his son, Isaac. We are grateful that our faith has room to name that struggle, and to wrestle with how we understand and interpret this ancient story. We come with minds and hearts that are open, and we invite the Spirit to breathe new life, and even surprise, into our image of God, we pray. Amen.

ENGAGING THE AKEDAH

Recruit four volunteers to read aloud Genesis 22:1-19, taking the roles of the narrator, God, Abraham, and Isaac. Ask those who aren't reading aloud to keep their Bibles closed for the time being. Alternatively, listen together to a recorded reading of the *Akedah.*

After the reading, discuss:

- What are your immediate reactions to and dominant impressions of this story?
- What language or images affected you most strongly, and why?
- Identify and briefly describe each major character in this story.
- What moment in this story do you identify as most important? Why?
- If asked to give this story a title, what would you title it?

WATCH THE VIDEO

Watch the session 2 video segment via DVD or Amplify Media. Invite responses and comments.

EXPLORING THE AKEDAH

Invite participants to open their Bibles to Genesis 22:1-19. Discuss:

- The story begins "[a]fter these things" (verse 1). Spend a few minutes scanning Genesis 12–21. To what "things" might the narrator be referring? How does reading this story within the larger context of Abraham's experiences to this point influence your understanding of it?
- The narrator says God "tested"—the Hebrew word can also be translated "tempted"—Abraham. "Does that feel off to you? God testing people?" asks Josh. How do you answer his question?
- Josh also asks, "Why is the clarification of exactly who Abraham is to sacrifice needed?" (verse 2). What do you think?
- How is God's call and Abraham's response in this story like and unlike God's call and Abraham's response in Genesis 12:1-4? How does God's command in this story appear to jeopardize God's promise in the earlier story? At what other points in the larger story of Abraham has the promise appeared threatened, and how did those threats resolve? (Consider 12:10-20; 14:14-16; 15:1-6; 16:1-6; 17:15-21; 20:1-7; 21:1-7.)
- What do you imagine Abraham and Sarah said, if anything—to each other, to themselves, to God—"in between" verses 2 and 3? Why do you suppose the story as we have it doesn't include these reactions and conversations?

- "Isaac unwittingly plays a role in his own horror story," writes Josh. How much or how little do you imagine Isaac knew about what was happening? Why do you think he carried the wood for the fire (verse 6)? What do you think of Abraham's response to his son's question (verses 7-8)?
- Josh states some traditions hold that Isaac is "somewhere around thirty-seven years old" in this story. How, if at all, does this possibility shape your reactions to and understanding of the Akedah?
- As Josh notes, Abraham says, "Here I am" three times in this story (verses 1, 7, 11). How are each of these occurrences similar and different? How else might Abraham have responded in each instance, and how might these different responses have changed the story?
- How does the refrain of "Here I am" echo throughout Scripture (Genesis 31:11; Exodus 3:4; 1 Samuel 3:4; Isaiah 6:8; Acts 9:10)? When and how, if ever, have you answered God with those words? When and how have you used them to answer other people?
- "The meaning [of this story] most readily available," writes Josh, "which I remember being taught at a young age, is that we should all be like Abraham, willing to sacrifice whatever God calls us to in order to be faithful." What, if anything, do you remember being told this story meant when you were young? What advantages does reading the story as one of faithful obedience to God offer? What problems does this reading present?
- "What kind of God demands the sacrifice of a child?" asks Josh. "What kind of father is commanded to sacrifice his child and he just does it?" What do you think about God as this story depicts God? What do you think about Abraham's willingness to obey God?
- Josh relates an ancient midrash (an ancient Jewish form of creatively engaging Scripture) that attributes to Mastêmâ,

a "prosecuting attorney" in the heavenly court, the idea of testing Abraham's faithfulness, much as Satan in the Book of Job wants to see Job's faithfulness tested. Does this midrash help you understand the story more or less, and why?

- Josh also notes "many Christians have immediately jumped to how a story like [the Akedah] might be fore-shadowing the Jesus experience." What details in the story support such a reading? Why does Josh believe it is important to engage the story "first and foremost as a story about Abraham and Isaac" rather than about Jesus? Do you agree with him? Why or why not?

- Josh writes that the story's "abrupt switch" at verse 11 from one source to another, seen in how the Deity's name shifts from "God" to "the LORD," suggests the story is about Abraham shifting his view of God: "The lesson Abraham learns…is that this God doesn't demand anything *from* him, but instead provides *for* him." What do you like and/or dislike about this interpretation? Do you believe God makes demands of us? Why or why not? Where in your own or others' experience can you point to God as provider?

CLOSING YOUR SESSION

Read aloud from *Bible Stories for Grown-Ups*: "I have come to see in this story of the near sacrifice of Isaac an invitation to Abraham, and to us, to open ourselves to changing our minds about God. . . . In a context in which gods were demanding and ruthless, a God who cares, sees, and provides generously is a massive step forward. It seems that this is how it works in the pages of Scripture and in the experience of our lives: God meets us where we are and invites us to take a step forward." Discuss:

- How have your views about God shifted over time? What are the earliest and/or most recent ways you have changed your mind about God, and what prompted those changes of mind?

- Josh suggests traumatic events, as the Akedah must have been, are also "potentially transformative" in our understanding of God, creating "fissures and cracks in our lenses that allow the possibility for us to see what has always been true, but what we had not yet noticed." To what extent has a traumatic event transformed your understanding of God? of yourself? of others?

- Josh concludes the Akedah invites us "to leave behind [a traumatic and inhumane] image of God, in order to embrace a better one." What practical, positive consequences would seeing God as "more expansive, compassionate, and inclusive than we thought possible" have in your own life? in the life of your congregation? in your community?

- What aspects of your image of God might God be calling you to leave behind? What aspects of that image might God call you to retain? How do you discern the difference?

CLOSING PRAYER

Give us wisdom, God, to discern your character and your voice. It can be scary and unsettling to leave behind the understandings and interpretations we have inherited or formed over years. Yet, we also trust that there is always going to be more to learn. We ask you to help us embrace the invitation, like Abraham, to journey into the unknown, trusting that you are leading us beyond visions that are too small and into a more expansive reality that has always been who you are. Amen.

SESSION 3

It's Not About the Fish: The Story of Jonah

SESSION OBJECTIVES

This session's readings and discussions will help participants:

- Reflect on advantages and disadvantages of particular and universal ways of looking at the world.
- Hear, read, and respond to the story of Jonah in new ways, paying special attention to the tensions it highlights between nationalist and universal approaches to faith.
- Rethink what implications faith in God has for the way we respond to our enemies.

BIBLICAL FOUNDATION

Then the LORD spoke to the fish, and it vomited Jonah out onto the dry land....

The word of the LORD came to Jonah a second time, saying, "Get up, go to Nineveh, that great city, and proclaim to it the message that I tell you." So Jonah set out and went to Nineveh, according to the word of the LORD. Now Nineveh was an exceedingly large city, a three days' walk across. Jonah began to go into the city, going a day's walk. And he cried out, "Forty days more, and Nineveh shall be overthrown!" And the people of Nineveh believed God; they proclaimed a fast, and everyone, great and small, put on sackcloth....

When God saw what they did, how they turned from their evil ways, God changed his mind about the calamity that he had said he would bring upon them, and he did not do it....

But this was very displeasing to Jonah, and he became angry. He prayed to the LORD and said, "O LORD! Is not this what I said while I was still in my own country? That is why I fled to Tarshish at the beginning, for I knew that you are a gracious and merciful God, slow to anger, abounding in steadfast love, and relenting from punishment. And now, O LORD, please take my life from me, for it is better for me to die than to live." And the LORD said, "Is it right for you to be angry?" Then Jonah went out of the city and sat down east of the city and made a booth for himself there. He sat under it in the shade, waiting to see what would become of the city.

The LORD God appointed a bush and made it come up over Jonah, to give shade over his head, to save him from his discomfort, so Jonah was very happy about the bush. But when dawn came up the next day, God appointed a worm that attacked the bush, so that it withered. When the sun rose, God prepared a sultry east wind, and the sun beat down on the head of Jonah so that he was faint and asked that he might die. He said, "It is better for me to die than to live."

But God said to Jonah, "Is it right for you to be angry about the bush?" And he said, "Yes, angry enough to die." Then the LORD said, "You are concerned about the bush, for which you did not labor and which you did not grow; it came into being in a night and perished in a night. And should I not be concerned about Nineveh, that great city, in which there are more than a hundred

*and twenty thousand persons who do not know their right hand
from their left and also many animals?"*

Jonah 2:10; 3:1-5, 10; 4:1-11

BEFORE YOUR SESSION

- Carefully read chapter 3 of *Bible Stories for Grown-Ups.*
  Note topics about which you have questions or want to
  do further research.
- Read the Book of Jonah several times, as well as
  background information from a trusted study Bible or
  commentary.
- Preview the session 3 video segment. Make notes to facilitate your group's discussion of it. Test your audiovisual
  equipment and/or capabilities for sharing your videoconference screen.
- Find images of a world map showing political boundaries
  and an image of the Earth as seen from space. Prepare to
  show these images to your group.
- You will need: Bibles for participants and/or on-screen
  slides to share, prepared with the biblical text; newsprint
  or markerboard; markers.

STARTING YOUR SESSION

Welcome participants. Show them the image of the world
map with political boundaries, and invite them to respond to it
with words or short phrases. Write responses on newsprint or
markerboard. Show them the image of the Earth as seen from
space, and invite responses. Write these responses on newsprint
or markerboard also. If possible, show the two images side by
side. Invite and write responses.

Discuss:

- Which of these images represents the way you most often think about the world? Why?
- When and how is each of these ways of looking at the world helpful? When and how is each limiting, or even harmful?
- How, if at all, can these views of the world complement and/or challenge each other?
- How does each of these views shape religious faith?

Tell participants this session considers what Josh calls "one of best-known stories from the Bible" and one that "conveys one of the central messages of Scripture," the story of Jonah. Suggest it is also a story about how the way in which we view the world shapes the way we consider God's relationship to us and to others.

OPENING PRAYER

God, the story of Jonah is familiar in both our memory and experience. This story has been told to us, and in so many ways experienced by us. Call us beyond the spectacular elements of this story and into what it might have to say to us in our own time and place today. Help us not sit in judgment over Jonah, but to enter into his shoes, that we may discover what he learned about you, we pray. Amen.

ENGAGING THE STORY OF JONAH

One of the Bible's shorter books, Jonah is fewer than 1,500 words in English translation and can be read aloud in under ten minutes. If time allows, so your group can consider the whole story, recruit participants to read Jonah 1–4 aloud, playing the roles of the narrator, God, Jonah, the sailors (Jonah 1), and the king of Nineveh (Jonah 3). If time is limited, summarize

Jonah 1:1–2:9 and then recruit volunteers to read aloud Jonah 2:10–4:11. Ask those who aren't reading aloud to keep their Bibles closed for the time being.

Alternatively, listen together to a recorded reading of Jonah. After the reading, discuss:

- What are your immediate reactions to and dominant impressions of this story?
- What language or images affected you most strongly, and why?
- Identify and briefly describe each major character in this story.
- What moment in this story do you identify as most important? Why?
- If asked to give this story a title, what would you title it?

WATCH THE VIDEO

Watch the session 3 video segment via DVD or Amplify Media. Invite responses and comments.

EXPLORING THE STORY OF JONAH

Invite participants to open their Bibles to Jonah. Discuss:

- Why does God call Nineveh a "great city" (1:2; 3:2)? How does the history Josh shares in chapter 3 help us understand Jonah's reluctance to go and preach there?
- How does Jonah's reluctance differ from the reluctance such prophets as Moses, Isaiah, and Jeremiah expressed?
- When, if ever, have you been reluctant to speak what you believed to be a message from God? When and how, if ever, have you tried to flee from God? What happened?
- Jonah's attempted escape to Tarshish reflects "a normal understanding of how things worked in the ancient world,"

writes Josh. "Deities were associated with places, and when you left that particular place and traveled into other territory, that [territory] might belong to a different god." How, if at all, do you find this understanding of "gods" (literal or otherwise) and places present in today's world?

- Compare and contrast Jonah's and the sailors' reactions to the storm (1:4-15). What details might have surprised this story's earliest audiences? When, if ever, has the piety and faith shown by people of other religious traditions impressed and instructed you?

- Josh states "the truth and power of [Jonah's] story does not rest in whether or not a human being was actually swallowed by a fish and subsequently spent three days and nights living in said fish." Do you agree? Why or why not?

- According to Josh, most scholars think Jonah's prayer (2:1-9) is a psalm that existed independently of the text because "it is not a prayer of repentance…but a prayer of thanksgiving for deliverance." How appropriate do you find this prayer for Jonah's circumstances, and why? How and when, if at all, do you use preexisting prayers, and why?

- What does God's second call to Jonah (3:1-2) suggest about God? about Jonah? What do you imagine might have happened had Jonah again tried to resist God's call? Why?

- How does Nineveh respond to Jonah's proclamation (3:5-9)? What does the scope of its response suggest about the way in which Nineveh is, indeed, "overthrown" (3:4)?

- How does God respond to Nineveh's repentance (3:10), and what do we learn about God's character? How does Jonah respond to God's response (4:1-3), and what do we learn about *his* character? Do you recognize yourself at all in Jonah's reaction? Why or why not?

- Jonah 4:2 echoes God's self-identification to Moses in Exodus 33:12-23. Read that Scripture. What connections can you make between the two stories, and how does each influence your understanding of the other?

- What lesson is God trying to teach Jonah through the shady bush, the worm that attacks it, and the hot wind (4:6-11)? Why do you think the narrator doesn't tell us how Jonah responded, opting instead for what Josh calls "an open-ended ending?" How do you imagine Jonah responded?

- Read Matthew 12:38-42 and Luke 11:29-32. What does Jesus say about Jonah in these Scriptures? How is Jonah a "sign" in Jesus's understanding? How does Jesus's view of Jonah's story, as presented in these passages, influence your own?

- Josh identifies "essentially two kinds of prophets" in the Bible: those who hold a "nationalist vision," and those who hold a "universal vision." Briefly describe each of these approaches. Why does Scripture contain prophetic writings that represent each (sometimes within the same book)? Do these two visions offer any perspective to each other, or are they mutually exclusive? Why? How do you see each vision reflected in approaches to faith today?

- "Historically," writes Josh, "we know that [Nineveh's repentance] didn't happen. Assyria didn't abandon their brutality." Do you think this historical record undermines or underscores the meaning and importance of Jonah's story? How so?

- "The author of Jonah uses him…to demonstrate the immense largeness of God's love, even for those we would deny, exclude, and erase." Who are people our society tends to try to "deny, exclude, and erase"? How do or how could you and your congregation demonstrate, in practical ways, God's love for these people?

CLOSING YOUR SESSION

Read aloud from *Bible Stories for Grown-Ups*: "The Book of Jonah calls us to see not just our own people—religion, nation, and so on—as worthy of love and care, but all humans, everywhere. It invites us to see our species, not just our group, as our responsibility." Discuss:

- Do you agree with Josh's conclusion about Jonah's meaning? Why or why not?
- What practical consequences follow from seeing "all humans, everywhere" as our responsibility? How, specifically, would or does such a view challenge and change the way you live your life? the way your congregation lives its life?
- Josh states that God's love, as depicted in Jonah, "calls us one step further: to rethink how we respond to our enemies." How will Jonah's story shape the way you deal with someone you consider an enemy—or who considers you to be his or her enemy?

CLOSING PRAYER

God, when our tables are too small, move us to expand them. When our compassion is exclusive and our mercy too narrow, may we hear the Spirit calling us to welcome, inclusion, and kindness. When, like Jonah, we choose to run from participation with you or allow our bitterness and anger to limit our understanding of your love, may we find ourselves overwhelmed by it so much that we can't help but share it. When we are swallowed up in our narrowness, may we be reminded of just how expansive your love for everyone and everything really is, we pray. Amen.

SESSION 4

Jesus in Unexpected Places: The Parable of the Talents

SESSION OBJECTIVES

This session's readings and discussions will help participants:

- Remember and appreciate the nature and power of storytelling.
- Explore the nature of parables and why Jesus told them.
- Hear, read, and respond to the parable of the talents in new ways, with special attention to the possibility that it depicts resistance to an exploitative economy and unjust social order.
- Identify practical things they and their congregations can do "to seek the flourishing of all human beings."

BIBLICAL FOUNDATIONS

When [Jesus] was alone, those who were around him along with the twelve asked him about the parables. And he said to them, "To you has been given the secret of the kingdom of God, but for those outside everything comes in parables, in order that

> 'they may indeed look but not perceive,
>   and may indeed hear but not understand;
> so that they may not turn again and be forgiven.' " …

With many such parables [Jesus] spoke the word to them as they were able to hear it; he did not speak to them except in parables, but he explained everything in private to his disciples.

Mark 4:10-12, 33-34

"For it is as if a man, going on a journey, summoned his slaves and entrusted his property to them; to one he gave five talents, to another two, to another one, to each according to his ability. Then he went away. At once the one who had received the five talents went off and traded with them and made five more talents. In the same way, the one who had the two talents made two more talents. But the one who had received the one talent went off and dug a hole in the ground and hid his master's money. After a long time the master of those slaves came and settled accounts with them. Then the one who had received the five talents came forward, bringing five more talents, saying, 'Master, you handed over to me five talents; see, I have made five more talents.' His master said to him, 'Well done, good and trustworthy slave; you have been trustworthy in a few things; I will put you in charge of many things; enter into the joy of your master.' And the one with the two talents also came forward, saying, 'Master, you handed over to me two talents; see, I have made two more talents.' His master said to him, 'Well done, good and trustworthy slave; you have been trustworthy in a few things; I will put you in charge of many things; enter into the joy of your master.' Then the one who had received the one talent also came forward, saying, 'Master, I knew that you were a harsh man, reaping where you did not sow and gathering where you did not scatter, so I was afraid, and I went and hid your talent in the ground. Here you have what is yours.' But his master replied, 'You wicked and lazy slave! You knew, did you, that I reap where I did not sow and gather where I did not scatter? Then you ought to have invested my money with the bankers, and on my return I would have received what was my own with interest. So take *the talent from him, and give it to the one with the ten talents. For to all those who have, more will be given, and they will have an abundance, but from those who have nothing, even what they have will be taken away. As for this worthless slave, throw him into the outer darkness, where there will be weeping and gnashing of teeth.'"*

Matthew 25:14-30

BEFORE YOUR SESSION

- Carefully read chapter 4 of *Bible Stories for Grown-Ups*. Note topics about which you have questions or want to do further research.
- Read the Biblical Foundations several times, as well as background information from a trusted study Bible or commentary.
- Preview the session 4 video segment. Make notes to facilitate your group's discussion of it. Test your audiovisual equipment and/or capabilities for sharing your videoconference screen.
- You will need: Bibles for participants and/or on-screen slides to share, prepared with the biblical text; newsprint or markerboard; markers.
- *Optional*: Write out a short fable, fairy tale, or other familiar story and remove selected nouns, verbs, adjectives, and adverbs.

STARTING YOUR SESSION

Welcome participants.

Option #1: Invite participants to play this storytelling game: One participant tells the first sentence of a fable, fairy tale, or other familiar story. Participants take turns continuing the story, one sentence at a time. On your turn, change something about the story. The group continues telling the story sentence by sentence, incorporating your change and making their own. Continue as long as participants enjoy the game or until the story naturally finishes.

Option #2: Ask participants, "Mad Libs"-style, for nouns, verbs, adjectives, and adverbs to fill in the blanks in your prepared written story. Don't read the story aloud until you have written down all responses; then do so, filling in the blanks in order for hopefully hysterical results.

Read aloud from *Bible Stories for Grown-Ups*: "Humans tell stories. It seems we are wired to craft narratives that allow us to express the inexpressible." Summarize Josh's memories of his grandfather who could make "familiar [stories]...new and exciting." Discuss:

- *(Optional):* How did you react to hearing and telling a familiar story in a new way during our game?
- Do you remember special storytellers from your childhood? If so, who were they? What makes them and their stories memorable?
- In what situations do you find yourself telling and/or listening to stories in your life now?
- What about stories makes them a suitable art for "express[ing] the inexpressible?"
- Josh writes about the first time he watched the movie *Grease* as an adult. He was surprised by content he didn't remember from childhood viewings. When and how have "familiar" stories surprised you on later hearings or viewings? How can revisiting "familiar" stories prove valuable?

Lead participants in brainstorming a list of Jesus's parables. Write responses on newsprint or markerboard. Tell participants the New Testament contains at least thirty of Jesus's parables (exact counts vary). How many did your group list?

Tell participants this session explores Jesus's purposes in telling parables and one of his most familiar parables, seeking unfamiliar but valuable meaning in it.

OPENING PRAYER

God, we ask for wisdom today as we engage one of Jesus's most well-known stories. May the image of God that we discover in this parable be worthy of you. Help us let go of any interpretation that fails to match your character. May we also hear the story of Jesus and the Kingdom today, and find new energy for collaborating with that vision in the world, we pray. Amen.

CONSIDERING JESUS THE STORYTELLER

Read aloud from *Bible Stories for Grown-Ups*: "Jesus was a prolific storyteller in his own right. He regularly taught in a kind of story called parables, narratives that invited hearers to grapple with the challenge and vision he was offering them." Discuss:

- What definitions and descriptions of parables have you heard in the past? Which did you find helpful or unhelpful, and why?
- Josh notes the word parable comes from the Greek parabola, "to cast alongside." How does this fact help us understand the nature of parables?
- "I think, for Jesus, parables were heavenly stories with earthly meanings," writes Josh. "Jesus uses parables to describe the kingdom of God, what it is like, and how it interacts with the world." What do you find helpful or unhelpful about this definition?

Recruit a volunteer to read aloud Mark 4:10-12, 33-34. Discuss:

- According to Mark, why did Jesus teach in parables?
- Do you think Jesus is *prescribing* or *describing* how "those outside" will react to his parables? Why?

- Why did Jesus need or want to privately explain his parables to his disciples? What does this fact suggest about the disciples? about Jesus's stories?
- Josh suggests Jesus's parables "describe the vision that Jesus seeks to bring to bear on the world." Review the group's list of Jesus's parables. Based on what you remember of these parables, what are some defining characteristics of Jesus's vision?

ENGAGING THE PARABLE OF THE TALENTS

Recruit volunteers to read aloud Matthew 25:14-30, taking the roles of the narrator (Jesus), the landowner, and the three enslaved men. Ask those who aren't reading aloud to keep their Bibles closed for the time being. Alternatively, listen together to a recorded reading of the parable.

After the reading, discuss:

- What are your immediate reactions to and dominant impressions of this story?
- What language or images affected you most strongly, and why?
- Identify and briefly describe each major character in this story.
- What moment in this story do you identify as most important? Why?
- If asked to give this story a title, what would you title it?

WATCH THE VIDEO

Watch the session 4 video segment via DVD or Amplify Media. Invite responses and comments.

EXPLORING THE PARABLE OF THE TALENTS

Invite participants to open their Bibles to Matthew 25:14-30. Discuss:

- As Josh notes, the landowner in the parable gives his enslaved workers enormous amounts of money to handle in his absence (verses 14-15). When was a time you were responsible for handling a large amount of someone else's money? How did that responsibility make you feel? How was your situation like and unlike that of the men in the story?

- What does the fact the landowner gave the three men money "each according to his ability" (verse 15) suggest about him? about the men?

- How favorable or unfavorable is your opinion of the third man, and why?

- "I find it interesting," writes Josh, "that the master… doesn't refute the image the [third] servant had of him." Why do you think the master does not?

- "The economy of Jesus's world was rigged in favor of the wealthiest in society," notes Josh, parenthetically adding, "[T]hings haven't changed all that much, have they?" Where do you see evidence of such economic "rigging" today?

- "In the end, the master evaluates the servant to be worthless. After all, if you aren't producing wealth to continue to expand the empire, what good are you?" When, if ever, have others decided your worth depends on how much wealth you can generate?

- Challenging a common interpretation of Jesus's parable, Josh asks, "Is God like this master? Really?" How do you answer?

- Josh suggests, "The master in this story isn't God," but "is more like a Caesar or Herod." How so? Do you agree?

- "[T]his third servant," writes Josh, "is acting as a whistleblower, calling out the injustice and inhumanity of the system and those who sustained it." When have you seen whistleblowers meet bad ends, as the third man in the parable does? Why are whistleblowers often "disposed of" as traitors instead of "praised" as heroes?

- Josh also suggests "the Jesus figure in the story...[is] none other than the third servant" because, like Jesus, the servant refuses to participate in an exploitative economy. Do you agree? Why or why not?

- Do you think all Jesus's parables contain a figure like God or Jesus? How might some of the parables the group listed earlier yield different meanings if they don't necessarily include a "Jesus figure"?

- How does the historical context of Matthew's Gospel—the aftermath of the Jewish war against Rome in 66-70 (see Matthew 24:1-2)—support or challenge Josh's suggestion that this parable is a warning against participation in an exploitative and unjust social order?

- Josh writes that Jesus's vision of the kingdom of God "was not a pie in the sky, heaven when you die vision, but a concrete, earthly vision. Jesus envisaged a world of justice and compassion, peace and equity, in which everyone had enough." Do you agree Jesus envisioned the world being this way? Why or why not?

CLOSING YOUR SESSION

Read aloud from *Bible Stories for Grown-Ups*: "To sum up the challenge of this parable in a sentence, I would say it is this: We must refuse to participate in the harm of others. Practically, this means living thoughtfully, embracing inconvenience when necessary to ensure the well-being of fellow humans, and using our voice, privilege, and resources to bring about a better world." Discuss:

- What are some practical, specific ways you have refused or are refusing to participate in the harm of others?
- As one practical response to the parable, Josh invites readers to think about how we spend our money: where and to whom it goes, and whether we spend it wisely. How would you grade your own wise, harm-avoiding use of money? Why? What factors can you and can you not control that would change how much your money helps or harms others?
- Josh also notes speaking out as allies to others who are being harmed can be scary. When have you spoken out on behalf of someone who needed an advocate? What happened? How do or can we move beyond fear to speak out when God would have us speak out?
- What is one specific area in which your congregation can do more, in Josh's words, "to seek the flourishing of all human beings"? How can you help make that congregational action come about?

CLOSING PRAYER

God, we hear Jesus's call to resist the ways of empire, and instead to find ourselves standing with and for those who have been oppressed and marginalized by it. May we not only do no harm, but may we work with you to bring about human flourishing for everyone, we pray. Amen.

SESSION 5

When Repentance Isn't Enough: Looking for Zacchaeus

SESSION OBJECTIVES

This session's readings and discussions will help participants:

- Hear, read, and respond to the story of Zacchaeus in new ways, with special attention to how Zacchaeus's encounter with Jesus is an experience of salvation.
- Compare and contrast the story of Zacchaeus with the story of Jesus's encounter with a rich ruler (Luke 18:18-23), and weigh questions raised about how human action can help or hinder God's "age to come."
- Discuss practical ways of responding to salvation by working to and helping to make wrong situations right for other people.

BIBLICAL FOUNDATIONS

[Jesus] entered Jericho and was passing through it. A man was there named Zacchaeus; he was a chief tax collector and was

45

rich. He was trying to see who Jesus was, but on account of the crowd he could not, because he was short in stature. So he ran ahead and climbed a sycamore tree to see him, because he was going to pass that way. When Jesus came to the place, he looked up and said to him, "Zacchaeus, hurry and come down, for I must stay at your house today." So he hurried down and was happy to welcome him. All who saw it began to grumble and said, "He has gone to be the guest of one who is a sinner." Zacchaeus stood there and said to the Lord, "Look, half of my possessions, Lord, I will give to the poor, and if I have defrauded anyone of anything, I will pay back four times as much." Then Jesus said to him, "Today salvation has come to this house, because he, too, is a son of Abraham. For the Son of Man came to seek out and to save the lost."

Luke 19:1-10

After this [Jesus] went out and saw a tax collector named Levi sitting at the tax-collection station, and he said to him, "Follow me." And he got up, left everything, and followed him.

Then Levi gave a great banquet for him in his house, and there was a large crowd of tax collectors and others reclining at the table with them. The Pharisees and their scribes were complaining to his disciples, saying, "Why do you eat and drink with tax collectors and sinners?" Jesus answered them, "Those who are well have no need of a physician but those who are sick; I have not come to call the righteous but sinners to repentance."

Luke 5:27-32

A certain ruler asked [Jesus], "Good Teacher, what must I do to inherit eternal life?" Jesus said to him, "Why do you call me good? No one is good but God alone. You know the commandments: 'You shall not commit adultery. You shall not murder. You shall not steal. You shall not bear false witness. Honor your father and mother.' " He replied, "I have kept all these since my youth." When Jesus heard this, he said to him, "There is still one thing *lacking. Sell all that you own and distribute the money to the poor, and you will have treasure in heaven; then come, follow me." But when he heard this, he became sad, for he was very rich. Jesus looked at him and said, "How hard it is for those who have wealth to enter the kingdom of God! Indeed, it is easier for a camel to go through the eye of a needle than for someone who is rich to enter the kingdom of God."*

Luke 18:18-25

BEFORE YOUR SESSION

- Carefully read Chapter 5 of *Bible Stories for Grown-Ups*. Note topics about which you have questions or want to do further research.
- Read the Biblical Foundations several times, as well as background information from a trusted study Bible or commentary.
- Preview the Session 5 video segment. Make notes to facilitate your group's discussion of it. Test your audiovisual equipment and/or capabilities for sharing your videoconference screen.
- You will need: Bibles for participants and/or on-screen slides to share, prepared with the biblical text; newsprint or markerboard; markers.

STARTING YOUR SESSION

Welcome participants. Ask:

- What's the biggest crowd you've even been a part of?
- When has a large crowd kept you from going where you wanted to go or seeing what you wanted to see?
- What are the greatest lengths to which you've gone to overcome a crowd that was an obstacle? Would you do so again? Why or why not?

Optional: Sing together the children's song Josh quotes near the beginning of Chapter 5 ("Zacchaeus Was a Wee Little Man"—should you need words, music, and hand motions, they are readily available online). Read aloud from *Bible Stories for Grown-Ups*: "The problem with this [song] is that it actually draws our attention away from the point of the story. The significance of Zacchaeus isn't his height, but his response to his encounter with Jesus."

Tell participants this session will consider how the story of Zacchaeus is about more than a man who had trouble seeing Jesus because of a crowd!

OPENING PRAYER

God, help us hear the story of Zacchaeus, and the invitation and challenge of it, through grown-up ears. May we resist the urge to assume or simply focus on minor details that, in the end, obscure the transformational experience that awaits us. May we enter into Zacchaeus's story, and may it change ours, we pray. Amen.

ENGAGING THE STORY OF ZACCHAEUS

Recruit volunteers to read aloud Luke 19:1-10, taking the roles of the narrator, Jesus, Zacchaeus, and two or three grumbling crowd members (verse 7). Ask those who aren't reading aloud to keep their Bibles closed for the time being. Alternatively, listen together to a recorded reading of the story.

After the reading, discuss:

- What are your immediate reactions to and dominant impressions of this story?
- What language or images affected you most strongly, and why?
- Identify and briefly describe each major character in this story.

- What moment in this story do you identify as most important? Why?
- If asked to give this story a title, what would you title it?

WATCH THE VIDEO

Watch the Session 5 video segment via DVD or Amplify Media. Invite responses and comments.

EXPLORING THE STORY OF ZACCHAEUS

Invite participants to open their Bibles to Luke 19:1-10. Discuss:

- This story takes place in Jericho. What other biblical associations does Jericho have (see Joshua 6; Luke 10:30)? How might these associations create expectations for what will happen in this story?
- Why would Jesus have been attracting a large crowd (verse 3)? Does Jesus still draw crowds today? If so, how? If not, why not?
- As Josh explains, tax collectors enforced Roman tax policies on their fellow Jews, charging "over and above" what was actually owed in order to make their own living. Given this context, how would most Jews in first-century Jericho likely have felt about a rich, "chief tax collector" (verse 2)?
- Luke doesn't tell us why Zacchaeus wanted to see Jesus. What do you imagine were his motives? Why do you think Luke says nothing about them?
- Josh wonders what Zacchaeus thought when he realized Jesus was talking to him (verse 5). What do you think? Why is Zacchaeus "happy to welcome" Jesus (verse 6)?
- Read Luke 5:27-32. As Josh notes, Jesus's meals with tax collectors like Levi and Zacchaeus caused controversy because, in the ancient world, sharing a meal with some-

one "was to make a statement about belonging, about equality." What is Jesus's response to those who object to his dinner companions? To what extent do shared meals still communicate belonging and equality today? What additional practices do?

- Josh doesn't think those who grumble at Jesus's choice "are bad, mean-spirited people," but "have been harmed by the Zacchaeuses of the world, and their reluctance toward Jesus's embrace of a tax collector is valid and understandable to say the least." Who might "the Zacchaeuses of the world" today be? Do you or your congregation raise any eyebrows or hackles because of your fellowship with them? If so, who, and why? If not, how might you start?

- How does Zacchaeus respond to Jesus inviting himself to dinner (verse 8)? What is the significance of his response (in the original Greek) being, as Josh notes, not in the future tense but in the present tense? Why does Zacchaeus repay "four times" the amount he has fraudulently gained (see Exodus 22:1)?

- Josh asks what Jesus's words in verses 9-10 "mean for how we think about salvation." How would you answer Josh's question?

- Citing the Exodus as the prime example, Josh states, "The overarching image of salvation in the Bible is not that of forgiveness, but of liberation." From what has Zacchaeus been freed? For what purpose has he been freed? Who else might experience liberation as a result of Zacchaeus's encounter with Jesus?

- How do you react to the idea that salvation is more about liberation than forgiveness? How, if at all, do the two images of salvation complement or challenge each other?

- "It seems so much of what Jesus does in the Gospels is grounded in calling people back to who they truly are"—in the case of Zacchaeus, "a son of Abraham" (verse 9). How are you and your congregation active in calling people back to their true identities?

- Who are "the lost" (verse 10) Jesus say he came to seek and save? How much or how little do you and your congregation talk about "the lost," and why?

- According to Josh, Zacchaeus's name means "pure" or "righteous." How is Zacchaeus's name ironic as this story begins? How ironic is it, if at all, by the story's end, and why?

- As Josh points out, this story occurs near the end of Luke's lengthy account of Jesus's "journey to Jerusalem" (9:51-19:44), where the values of God's kingdom will "confront and clash with the values of the empire in dramatic fashion, leaving Jesus nailed to a Roman cross." How does this context influence your response to and understanding of the story?

ENCOUNTERING THE RICH RULER

Recruit volunteers to read aloud Luke 18:18-25, taking the roles of the narrator, Jesus, and the rich ruler. Ask those who aren't reading aloud to keep their Bibles closed for the time being. Alternatively, listen together to a recorded reading of the story.

After the reading, have participants turn in their Bibles to the story. Lead them in a brainstorming session in which they compare and contrast this story with the story of Zacchaeus. Write responses on newsprint or markerboard.

Discuss:

- Josh says the rich man is not asking, "How do I go to heaven when I die?," but how he can be sure he has a place in the "age to come" of justice and peace. How might the two questions reveal different priorities? What does the image of "inheritance" suggest about the nature of "eternal life" (verse 18)? What impression does the question the man asks give you of him?

- How do you react to Jesus's questioning the man calling him good (verse 19)?

- "Perhaps," Josh wonders, the man's question "was less about what he should do" and more about wanting "affirmation." How, if at all, would this motivation affect your attitude toward the man? When and how do you seek affirmation from others? How do we tell the difference between beneficial and harmful ways of seeking others' affirmation?

- How do you imagine Jesus expected the man to react to the challenge in verse 22? Why?

- Josh notes Jesus omits "the commands that deal with interpersonal relationships" in his initial response to the man, but then seems to suggest the man's personal fortune violates the command against coveting: "When the vast, overwhelming majority lives below a subsistence level, ... amassing wealth isn't an activity that is neutral in impact." How do you assess the moral impact of the ways you generate income and accumulate wealth? How does your congregation evaluate the impact of its money and possessions?

- "Jesus isn't creating a hoop for the rich ruler to jump through," writes Josh; "he's drawing his attention to the truth that the rich man's own actions are making the world he claims to long for a present impossibility." How do you respond to this interpretation? How do we know which of our actions, if any, make God's "age to come" a "present impossibility?" Where do we find the will and strength to act differently?

- In Mark (10:22) and Matthew (19:22), the man sadly goes away. In Luke (18:23-24), he does not. Do you find this difference significant? If so, why? If not, why not?

- What do you imagine the rich man and Zacchaeus would say to each other if they met after their respective encounters with Jesus?

CLOSING YOUR SESSION

Read aloud from *Bible Stories for Grown-Ups*: "It's clear that Zacchaeus knows he's caused harm to others, and he commits to making it right by paying reparations up to four times the amount he defrauded. The encounter with Jesus transformed Zacchaeus in real and practical ways."

Discuss:

- "God will not impose the 'age to come,'" states Josh. Do you agree? Why or why not?
- Josh writes of his uncomfortable realization that "while I've been waiting for God to do something about the world's problems, God has actually been waiting for me." What is one of the world's problems you, personally, are doing real and practical things to help make better? How? What about your congregation?
- "Every iniquity and injustice that exist on this planet is a humanly created problem," writes Josh, "and at the same time, the solution to these problems will come from us." What role, if any, does God play in solving these human problems?
- As Josh points out, "Zacchaeus repents, but…[his] repentance leads to repair." When, if ever, have you experienced this connection between repentance and repair? Where might God be calling you to be an agent of repair today?
- How would you respond to someone who says, "Only God can make the world the way it should be, and not all the good works we can do can save us"?

CLOSING PRAYER

God, we see in the story of Zacchaeus a call to bring the Kingdom into our reality, on earth as it is in heaven. We also hear an invitation to go beyond just words, and to rearrange our lives in meaningful ways to make that vision a reality in our own lives and communities. Give us the courage and strength to do so, we pray. Amen.

SESSION 6

Updating Our Lenses: Healing the Man Who Was Blind

SESSION OBJECTIVES

This session's readings and discussions will help participants:

- Articulate their thoughts and feelings about miracles of Jesus recorded in the Gospels, and about the possibility of miracles today.
- Hear, read, and respond in new ways to two stories of Jesus's miracles: restoring sight to a man who was blind, and casting a dangerous spirit out of a boy.
- Define the "Messianic Secret" motif in Mark's Gospel and ponder its significance, especially in the context of the story of Peter's confession of faith.
- Reflect on how their understanding of and faith in Jesus has changed over time and seek support for their continuing growth in understanding and faith from their congregation.

BIBLICAL FOUNDATIONS

[Jesus and the disciples] came to Bethsaida. Some people brought a blind man to him and begged him to touch him. He took the blind man by the hand and led him out of the village, and when he had put saliva on his eyes and laid his hands on him, he asked him, "Can you see anything?" And the man looked up and said, "I can see people, but they look like trees, walking." Then Jesus laid his hands on his eyes again, and he looked intently, and his sight was restored, and he saw everything clearly. Then he sent him away to his home, saying, "Do not even go into the village."

Mark 8:22-26

Jesus went on with his disciples to the villages of Caesarea Philippi, and on the way he asked his disciples, "Who do people say that I am?" And they answered him, "John the Baptist; and others, Elijah; and still others, one of the prophets." He asked them, "But who do you say that I am?" Peter answered him, "You are the Messiah." And he sternly ordered them not to tell anyone about him.

Then he began to teach them that the Son of Man must undergo great suffering and be rejected by the elders, the chief priests, and the scribes and be killed and after three days rise again. He said all this quite openly. And Peter took him aside and began to rebuke him. But turning and looking at his disciples, he rebuked Peter and said, "Get behind me, Satan! For you are setting your mind not on divine things but on human things."

Mark 8:27-33

Someone from the crowd answered [Jesus], "Teacher, I brought you my son; he has a spirit that makes him unable to speak, and whenever it seizes him, it dashes him down, and he foams and grinds his teeth and becomes rigid, and I asked your disciples to cast it out, but they could not do so." He answered them, "You faithless generation, how much longer must I be with you? How much longer must I put up with you? Bring him to me."

And they brought the boy to him. When the spirit saw him, immediately it convulsed the boy, and he fell on the ground and rolled about, foaming at the mouth. Jesus asked the father, "How long has this been happening to him?" And he said, "From childhood. It has often cast him into the fire and into the water, to destroy him; but if you are able to do anything, help us! Have compassion on us!" Jesus said to him, "If you are able! All things can be done for the one who believes." Immediately the father of the child cried out, "I believe; help my unbelief!"

Mark 9:17-24

BEFORE YOUR SESSION

- Carefully read chapter 6 of *Bible Stories for Grown-Ups*. Note topics about which you have questions or want to do further research.
- Read the Biblical Foundations several times, as well as background information from a trusted study Bible or commentary.
- Preview the session 6 video segment. Make notes to facilitate your group's discussion of it. Test your audiovisual equipment and/or capabilities for sharing your videoconference screen.
- You will need: Bibles for participants and/or on-screen slides to share, prepared with the biblical text; newsprint or markerboard; markers.

STARTING YOUR SESSION

Welcome participants. Lead your group in brainstorming a list of Jesus's miracles as recorded in the Gospels. Write responses on newsprint or markerboard. Discuss:

- Do you have a favorite story of Jesus's miracles? If so, which one and why?

- Do you generally accept that Jesus's miracles happened as the Gospels narrate them? Why or why not?
- Why do the Gospels include stories about Jesus's miracles? If the Gospels did not include these stories, how, if at all, do you imagine their absence would change your attitude toward Jesus?
- Have you experienced miracles in your life? Do you know others who have had miraculous experiences?
- Following John's Gospel, Josh suggests Jesus's miracles are "signs" "attempting to draw our attention somewhere...[They] always point beyond themselves and to the larger mission and message of Jesus." If you like this idea, why? If not, why not?

Tell participants this session will explore two stories of Jesus's miracles, and how they might help us focus more clearly on Jesus's mission and message.

OPENING PRAYER

God, as we experience a story of Jesus performing a sign, may we remain open to where it's pointing. As we explore this wonder, may it open us up, moving us beyond our assumptions and forward on the path of transformation, we pray. Amen.

ENGAGING THE STORY

Recruit three volunteers to read aloud Mark 8:22-26, taking the roles of the narrator, Jesus, and the man who was blind. Ask those who aren't reading aloud to keep their Bibles closed for the time being. Alternatively, listen together to a recorded reading of the story.

After the reading, discuss:

- What are your immediate reactions to and dominant impressions of this story?

- What language or images affected you most strongly, and why?
- Identify and briefly describe each major character in this story.
- What moment in this story do you identify as most important? Why?
- If asked to give this story a title, what would you title it?

WATCH THE VIDEO

Watch the session 6 video segment via DVD or Amplify Media. Invite responses and comments.

EXPLORING A STORY OF SIGHT RESTORED

Invite participants to open their Bibles to Mark 8. Discuss:

- Josh notes "an anonymous group helped facilitate" an encounter between the man who was blind and Jesus (verse 22). How have communities facilitated your own encounters with Jesus? When have you been part of communities that facilitate others' encounters with him?
- Why does Jesus lead the man out of Bethsaida (verse 23) before attempting to heal his blindness?
- Josh notes a legend about the Emperor Vespasian having "healed a man who was blind by spitting upon his eyes." What messages might Mark be communicating in telling a similar story about Jesus?
- Why is the man unable to see perfectly clearly after Jesus first touches his eyes (verses 23-24)? What do you think about Josh's suggestion that Mattthew and Luke, who do not tell a version of this story, "didn't like the optics of Jesus being unable to heal this man on the first try"?

- Why does Jesus tell the man to avoid the village on his way home (verse 26)?

CONTEMPLATING THE MESSIANIC SECRET

Read aloud from *Bible Stories for Grown-Ups*: "In the Gospel of Mark scholars have noticed a recurring pattern in which Jesus regularly tries to keep his wonder-working activity off the radar." Give participants a few minutes to skim Mark looking for examples of this "Messianic Secret" motif. (Josh gets them started, citing several examples in Mark 1 alone.) List occurrences participants find on newsprint or markerboard. Discuss:

- Why do you think Jesus tries to keep his "Messianic Secret" in Mark?
- Read or review Josh's explanation of what the term messiah (Hebrew for "anointed one") meant for many Jews in Jesus's day. How might this term's religious and political significance help make sense of the "Messianic Secret"?

Recruit volunteers to read aloud Mark 8:27-33, taking the roles of the narrator, Jesus, the disciples, and Peter. Discuss:

- How does this story's setting in "the villages of Caesarea Philippi" (verse 27)—the name, Josh explains, is "an homage to both a Roman Caesar... and a son of Herod the Great"—help us appreciate how Jesus understood his messianic identity?
- Why does Jesus want to know who people say he is? Why does he want to know who his disciples say he is?
- Why does Peter rebuke Jesus? Why does Jesus rebuke Peter? Why does he refer to Peter as "Satan"?

- How does this story reinforce the "Messianic Secret" pattern while helping us define what the idea of "Messiah" meant for Jesus?
- How, if at all, does or should the "Messianic Secret" shape the way those who proclaim Jesus as Messiah today view themselves and act toward others?

EXPLORING A STORY OF AN EXORCISM

Recruit volunteers to read aloud Mark 9:17-24 (or 9:14-29), taking the roles of the narrator, Jesus, the father of the boy, the disciples, and the crowd. Discuss:

- How do you react to Bible stories about possession by spirits? Do you believe possessions like this happen today? Why or why not?
- When, if ever, have you felt as helpless as the father in this story must feel (verses 17-18, 21-22)? What did or do you do when you feel such helplessness?
- Why do you think Jesus's disciples were unable to cast the spirit out of the boy (verses 18, 28-29)?
- The father tells Jesus, "I believe; help my unbelief!" (verse 24). Which half of his declaration do you agree with most days? Why? How do you believe God responds to you when you feel you have more "unbelief" than "belief"?
- "Jesus's statement about 'all things' being possible for the person with faith," writes Josh, "seems really out of reach for me most days." What about you?
- Earlier in chapter 6, Josh tells the story of a friend in seminary who said, "When I could no longer pray, I let the Church pray for me." How much or how little can you relate to his friend's experience, and why? How does

your community of faith encourage those members who feel they need "help" with their "unbelief"?

- Josh asks, "Is it possible that the longing for faith is what having faith is all about"? What do you think? Why?

CLOSING YOUR SESSION

Josh suggests Mark uses the story of the healing in Bethsaida and the stories around it to depict the disciples gradually coming to "see" who Jesus was and why he had come. Read aloud from *Bible Stories for Grown-Ups*: "The truth is we are always in process.... To be alive and human is to be in a continual state of learning to see.... In this tradition we are all learners, there are no experts.... What if the journey forward is actually the point? What if there is no other way forward than the sometimes-clumsy path of learning and growing over time"? Discuss:

- How did the disciples' experience of the first Easter change their understanding of and faith in Jesus? Do you think it was easier, harder, or about the same for Jesus's first followers to have faith in him, and why?
- What are the most significant ways your understanding of Jesus has changed over time? What, if anything, about your understanding of Jesus has not changed over time?
- What is one aspect of your faith, if any, in which you feel you are currently on a "clumsy path" forward? How can your congregation and this study group help you on your journey?

Thank participants for sharing this six-session study of *Bible Stories for Grown-Ups* with you. Invite volunteers to talk briefly about one or two key insights or realizations, or continuing questions, from the study that they believe will influence their faith most in the days, weeks, and years ahead.

CLOSING PRAYER

God, give us patience, knowing that we are on a journey. We know this path of transformation isn't a quick fix or a call to image maintenance. We are grateful that "I believe, help my unbelief" is enough, and we invite you to meet us in that space and by your Spirit lead us forward. Amen.

Watch videos based on *Bible Stories for Grown-Ups: Reading Scripture with New Eyes* with Josh Scott through Amplify Media.

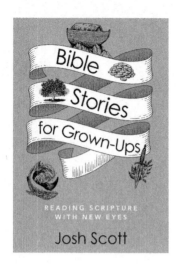

Amplify Media is a multimedia platform that delivers high quality, searchable content with an emphasis on Wesleyan perspectives for churchwide, group, or individual use on any device at any time. In a world of sometimes overwhelming choices, Amplify gives church leaders and congregants media capabilities that are contemporary, relevant, effective and, most importantly, affordable and sustainable.

With *Amplify Media* church leaders can:

- Provide a reliable source of Christian content through a Wesleyan lens for teaching, training, and inspiration in a customizable library
- Deliver their own preaching and worship content in a way the congregation knows and appreciates
- Build the church's capacity to innovate with engaging content and accessible technology
- Equip the congregation to better understand the Bible and its application
- Deepen discipleship beyond the church walls

Printed in Great Britain
by Amazon

20555763R00037